THE WORLD OF TILION

THE COLORING BOOK

Volume One

The World of Tilion Official Coloring Book, Volume 1

For information address Niveus Press
328 N Main St., Sellersville, PA

Printed in the USA

First Edition, January 2025
10 9 8 7 6 5 4 3 2 1

www.susanlmarkloff.com

ISBN 978-1-956542-30-1

NIVEUS PRESS
Called to the In-Between

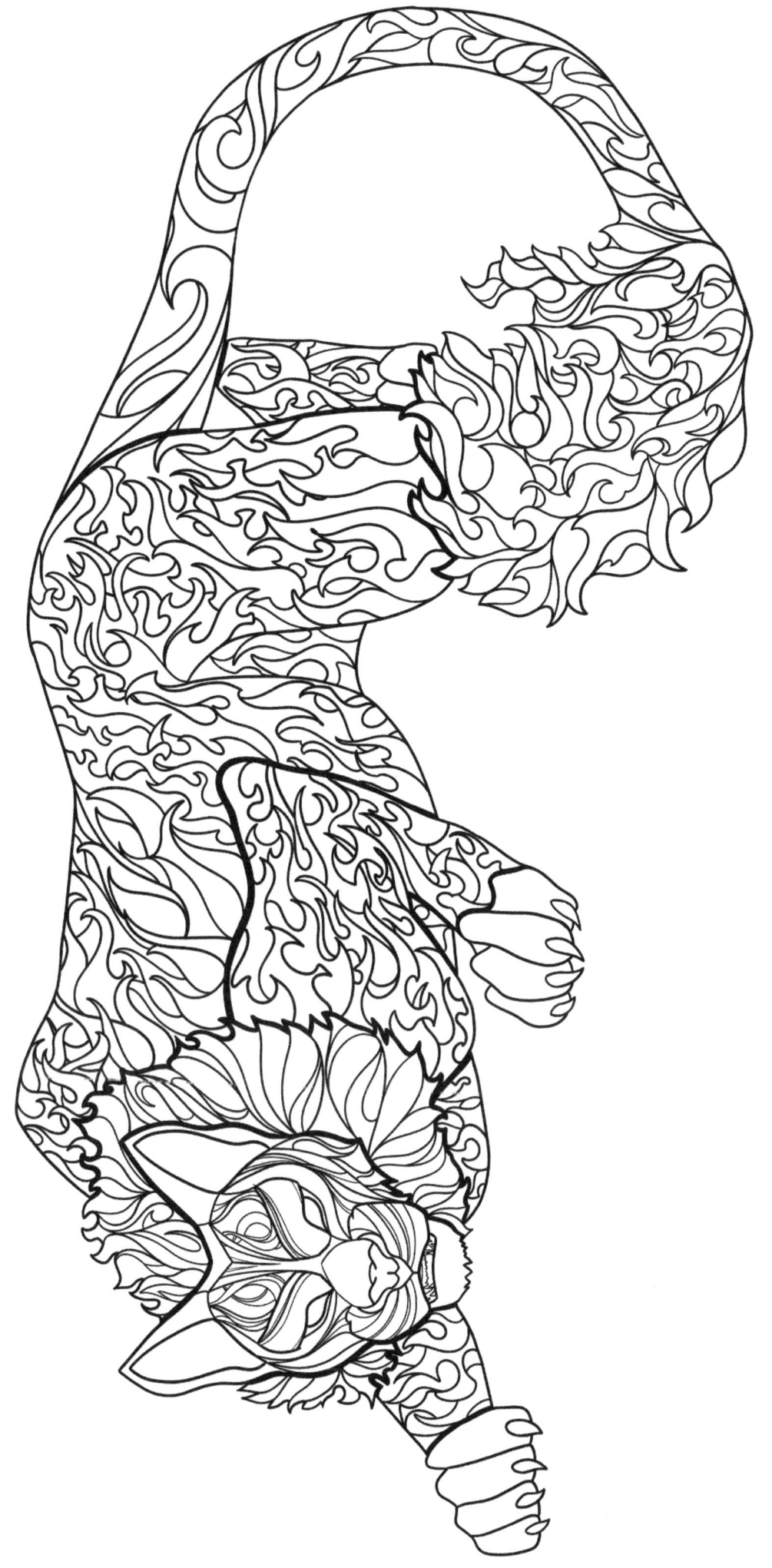

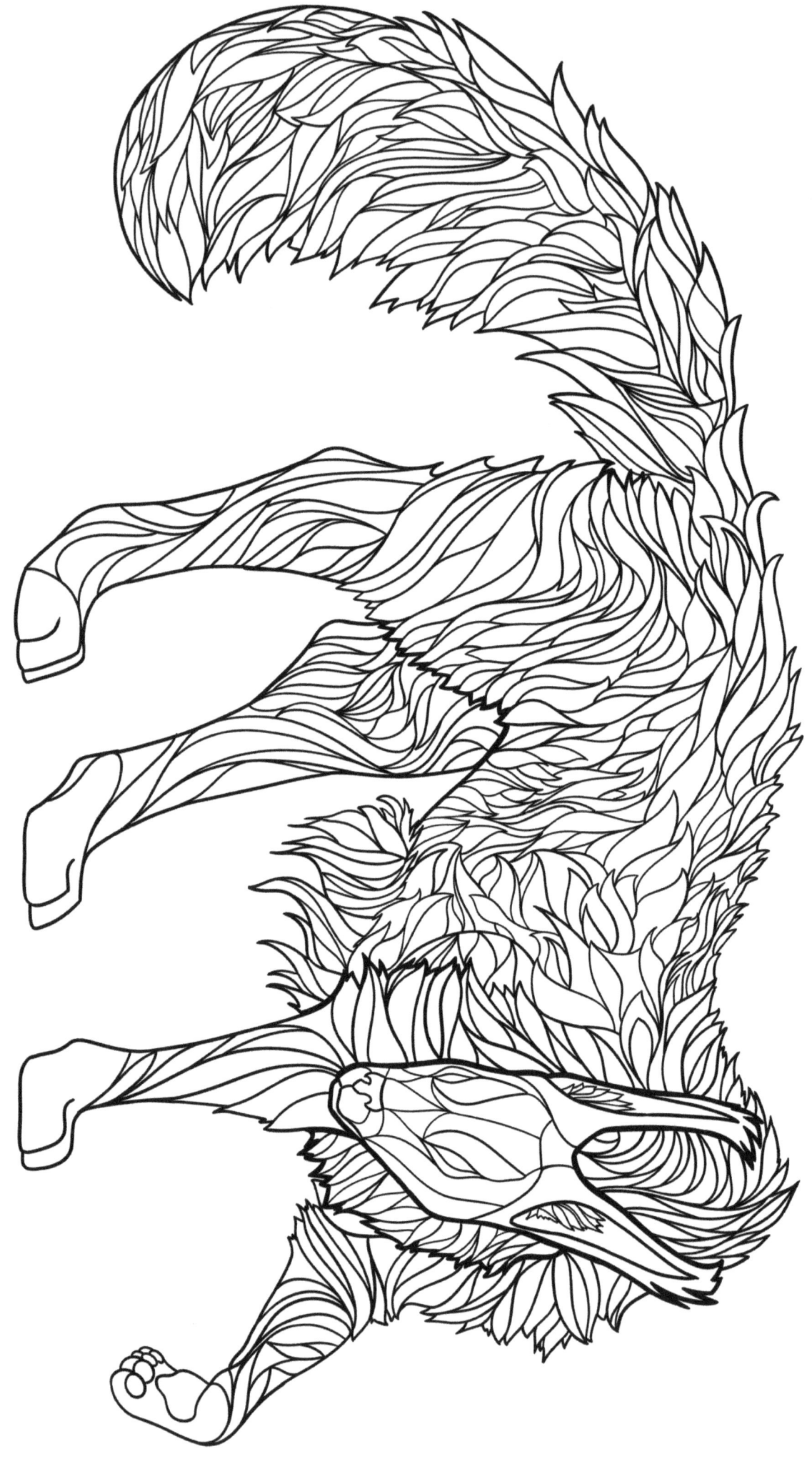

HBE Logo ©2021 Niveus Press

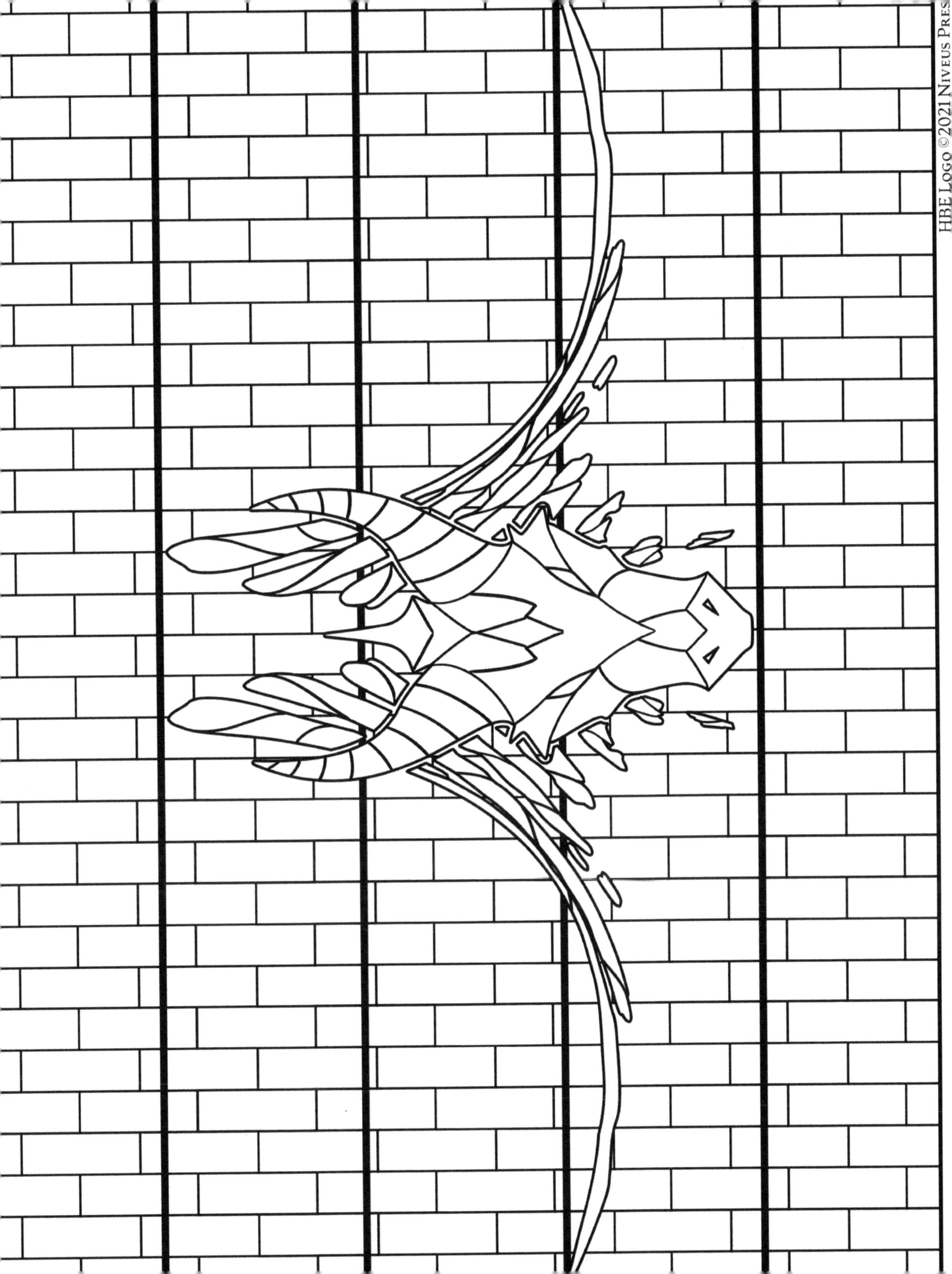

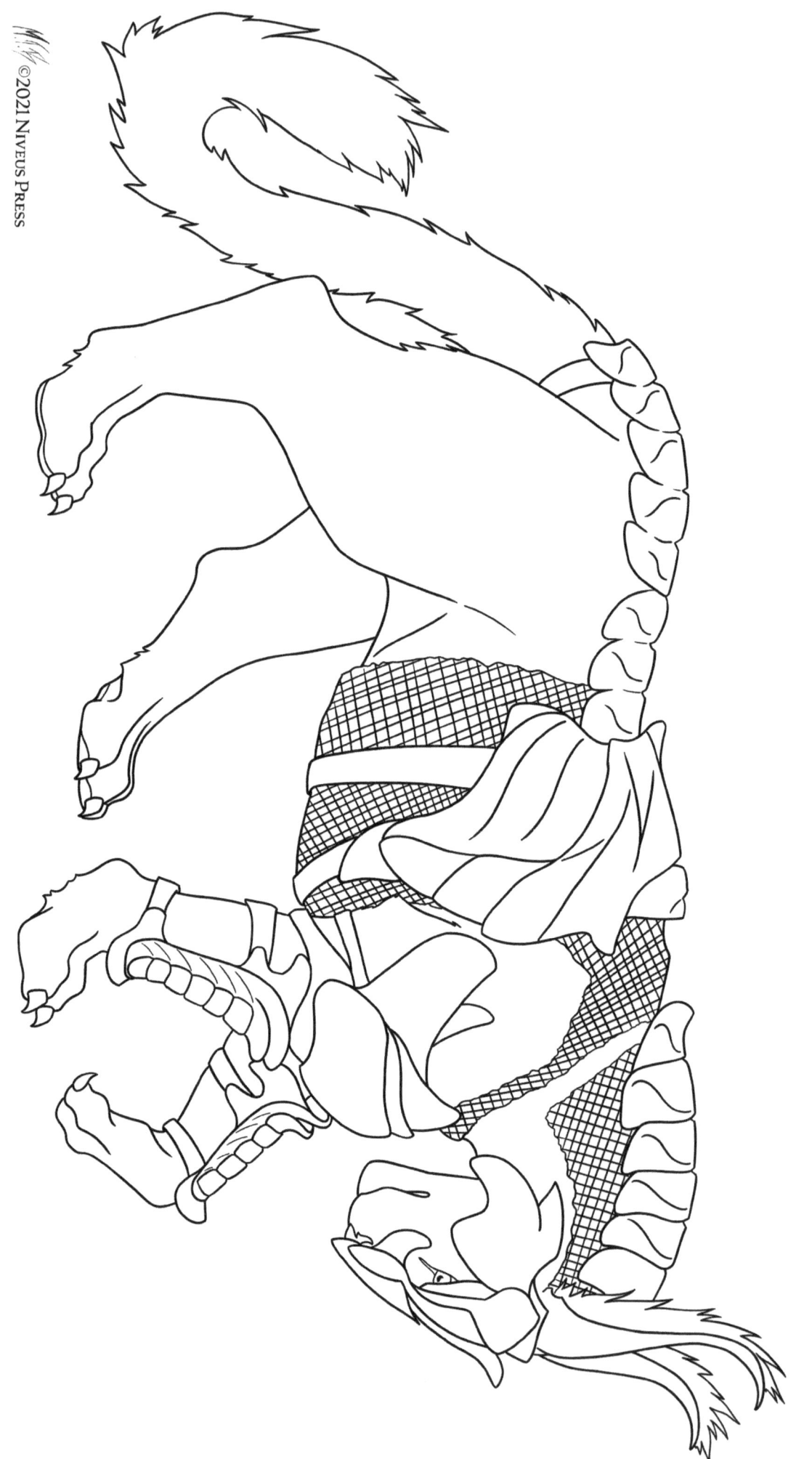

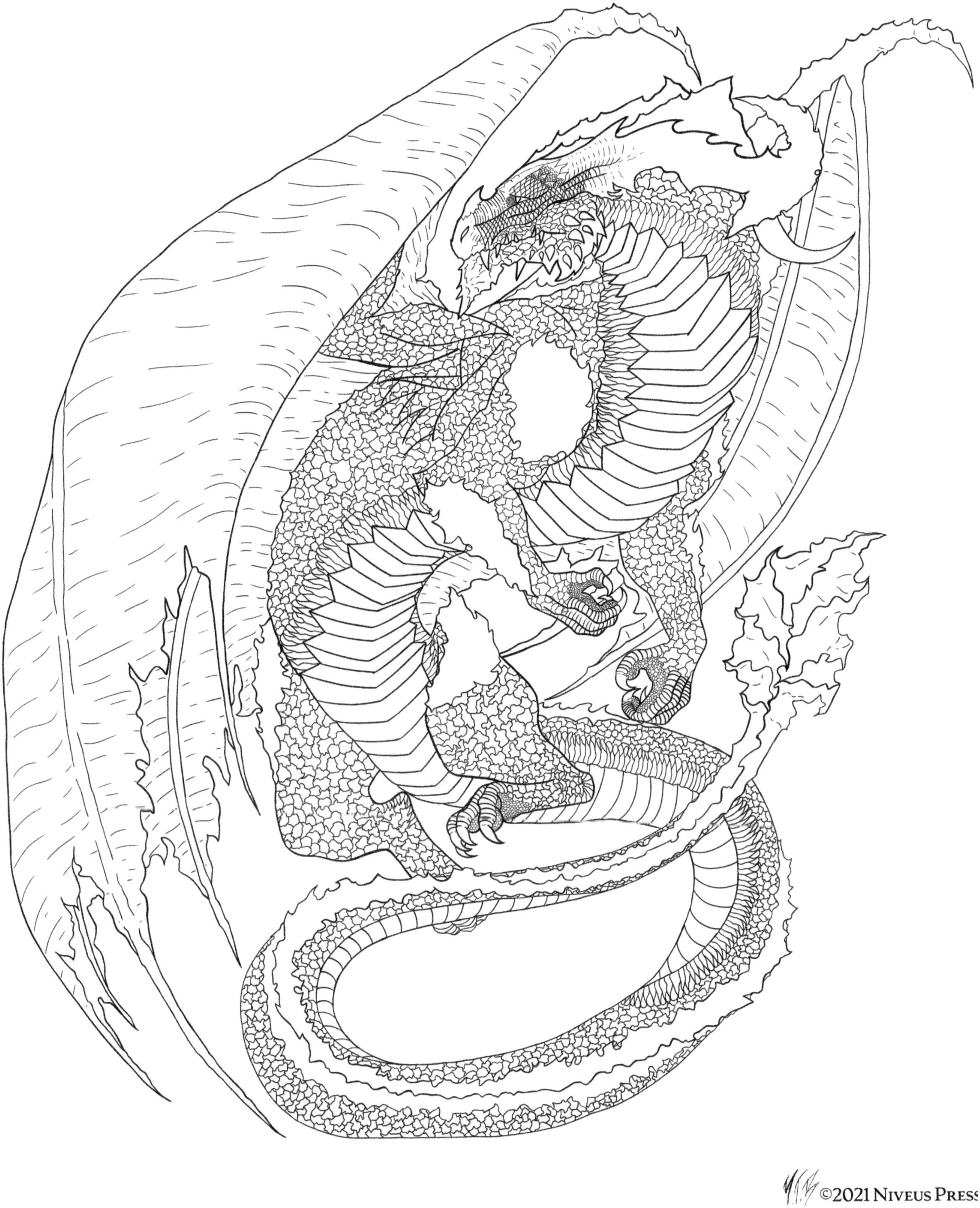

©2021 Niveus Press

CHLOE
GRACE
ARTIST

CHLOE
GRACE
ARTIST

CHLOE
GRACE
ARTIST

CHLOE
GRACE
ARTIST